Just STOP... and THINK!

A Lucky Duck Book

Just STOP...

and THINK!

Helping Children Plan to Improve Their Own Behaviour

Second Edition

Fiona Wallace

P·C·P

Paul Chapman
Publishing

Paul Chapman Publishing
A SAGE Publications Company
1 Oliver's Yard
55 City Road
London EC1Y 1SP

SAGE Publications Inc.
2455 Teller Road
Thousand Oaks, California 91320

SAGE Publications India Pvt Ltd
B 1/I 1 Mohan Cooperative Industrial Area
Mathura Road, New Delhi 110 044

SAGE Publications Asia-Pacific Pte Ltd
33 Pekin Street #02-01
Far East Square
Singapore 048763

www.luckyduck.co.uk

Illustrator: Philippa Drakeford
Activity sheets designed by: Nick Shearn

A catalogue record for this book is available from the British Library

ISBN 978 1 4129 2898 4

Library of Congress Control Number: 2006932492

Typeset by C&M Digitals (P) Ltd, Chennai, India
Printed in India by Replika Pvt, Ltd
Printed on paper from sustainable resources

A big thank you to all the pupils who have allowed
me to help them improve their own behaviour.
Go for it.

Contents

Introduction

Children who struggle with their behaviour, just like those who struggle with an academic task such as learning to read or perform maths calculations, need extra, regular, structured help from adults in school to build on the skills already mastered. With both learning and behaviour difficulties, time should be spent with the pupil looking at the skills they already have and agreeing targets for the future. Just as when working to improve an academic skill, a structured programme of support needs to be put in place to *teach* the appropriate behaviours.

This book provides a ready-made set of materials for staff working with pupils who are experiencing difficulty in school with their behaviour:

- to look at the current situation
- to explore the range of possible ways forward
- to draw up an action plan and record and review progress.

This book could be used in conjunction with two companion publications, *Not You Again!* and *What Else Can I Do With You?*, which focus on improving or removing particular playground and classroom behaviours. However, in contrast to the materials in the first two books, those in *Just Stop... and Think!* are not linked to any specific problem behaviour. They can be used for a wide range of difficulties, from the acting-out behaviours so familiar to teachers of late primary/early secondary pupils, to the more withdrawn behaviours shown by some pupils under great emotional stress. Some of the principles that guided the development of all three books are listed below:

- Adults can help children improve their behaviour without resorting to punishment or to strategies based on lost learning opportunities.

- Staff should be able to deal effectively with a child in trouble without automatically attributing blame to the child or their actions.

- Children should take responsibility for their actions ... both those that get them into trouble and those that they can take to change their behaviour for the better. The worksheets provide a set of activities that encourage children to think about themselves in a constructive and critical manner and then to plan improvements.

- No child should be written off as beyond help and neither is any child perfect. There is always the chance to learn new skills and strengthen existing positive behaviours and relationships.

- Resources for teachers must be easy to use. These sheets only need copying and this can be done freely within the purchasing establishment.

Before you start

A solution-focused, brief therapy model of helping reminds us that any step in the right direction, however small, is worth encouraging and that the 'client' always has at least part of their solution available to them. It also reminds us not to take control and direct the way in which a difficulty could be resolved. Our aim should be to help the pupil find their own solution rather than for us to become an expert on their problem. When using these materials our role is to support the pupil in exploring the situation they find themselves in. Instead of dwelling on past problems, we should try to keep the focus on learning from what has happened and putting those lessons into practice for future improvement. We should try to help pupils see what they already know about their difficulties and potential solutions then guide them in opening up possibilities that will help them move forward. Above all, we must remember that it is the problem that needs solving, not the pupil!

The language we use when working through these sheets is important if we are to remain as advisers and not become directors. It is very hard not to slip into the 'I'm the expert on your behaviour' role. It is hard not to launch into saying things like 'You need to ...' 'You should try...' 'If I were you ...'.

Many of the things we would usually say can be re-phrased to fit a solution-focused approach. Try versions of these:

- What would you like to change?
- What is different since we last met?
- When does the problem happen less/not happen? Why?
- How will you know when things are starting to get better?
- What will other people notice as things improve?
- What do you think you should do more of?
- If this is the worst things can be, what are you doing to keep yourself going?
- What would people notice if the problem went away?
- What would they/you be doing that was different?
- What have you learned that might help you?
- How will I know if this session has been useful to you?

The pupils' answers to questions like these will begin to open up a range of possible ways forward. But, before coming up with a list of things to do, it is important to help youngsters reflect on where they are now and where they would like to be so that they can form a realistic view of the progress to be made. Scaling questions are useful here. For example:

- On a scale of 1 (the pits) to 10 (perfection!) where are you now?
- Why are you at that point?

- How will you know when you have moved one point (or more) up?

- What point of the scale do you want to be at?

Once a realistic point to aim for has been agreed then we can begin to help the pupil plan how best to move in that direction, using their own suggestions for progress markers along the way.

How To Use the CD-ROM

The CD-ROM contains a PDF file, labelled 'Worksheets.pdf' which contains worksheets and session record sheet. You will need Acrobat Reader version 3 or higher to view and print these resources.

The documents are set up to print to A4 but you can enlarge them to A3 by increasing the output percentage at the point of printing using the page set-up settings for your printer.

How to use this book

The materials in this book are grouped in several sections aimed at helping youngsters to:

- Understand their own behaviour
- See others' point of view
- Think about how the future might look
- Consider the range of choices for action
- Be aware of potential help and pitfalls
- Plan a course of action
- Check and review their progress.

However much staff would like to spend unlimited time helping pupils analyse a situation, learn from it and plan a way forward, time in the busy school day is going to be limited. A 15–20 minute session should be enough to work through each of the sheets. The emphasis is on doing something today, next lesson, and not on spending hours thinking and prevaricating about taking the first few difficult steps. Remember any step in the right direction is to be celebrated and encouraged. Some may need more than one session if there is a suggested activity linked to the sheet. All could have a follow-up session to help the pupil review their progress and plan what to do next but this may need to be the pupil's choice.

Your time together might go something like this:

Hello, how are you? Establish a rapport with the pupil to help them feel you are on their side, at least for the next 20 minutes!

What's new? Ask what has happened that is helpful since you agreed to meet ... last met ... the outburst in class ... The idea is to help the pupil see that they can make changes by themselves, that they already have part of the solution to their predicament ... and that you do not need to make the changes for them.

Moving on. This will be the main work of the session using one of the sheets. If possible develop ideas suggested by the pupil that have already begun to work for them.

Winding up. Remind yourself and the pupil of the key points of the session, in particular the action plan. Agree if, and when, you need to meet again.

Record keeping

Those pupils for whom sessions using these resources are appropriate may well be 'on the Code of Practice' or receiving targeted support as part of a Pastoral Support Programme (PSP). A record will need to be kept of help given and plans made. The pupil should be encouraged to keep their sheet as a reminder of issues discussed and the things they are going to do. If the pupil wishes to put his or her name on the sheet then OK but this should not be insisted upon. If the work is lost then it should not draw attention to the pupil when found. However, staff will need to keep some record of the session, perhaps toward a review of the pupil's Individual Behaviour Plan (IBP). The record sheet at the end of this section following page xiii can be freely photocopied and allows staff to note the issues raised, the plans made and any reminders for areas to explore in future meetings.

Be creative with the pupils you work with! Use these materials in any way you feel would be helpful to the pupil.

Further reading and resources

There are, of course, numerous resources, both printed and online, addressing problem behaviour in the classroom and other settings. The *Incentive Plus* catalogue is an excellent starting point. It is full of posters, games, books and other resources in the area of behaviour and emotional literacy.

Incentive Plus   Tel. (UK) 01908 526120
6 Fernfield Farm   www.incentiveplus.co.uk
Little Horwood
Milton Keynes
MK17 0PR

The companion volumes to this one address specific difficulties. Many of the photocopiable activities in *Not You Again*! by Fiona Wallace and Diane Caesar will help the child struggling with appropriate playtime and lunchtime behaviour. *What Else Can I Do With You*? by Fiona Wallace provides a range of activities, also photocopiable, aimed at helping children improve their classroom behaviour. Both are published by Lucky Duck at www.luckyduck.co.uk.

Those of you who want to know more about solution-focused brief therapy (SFBT) might like to browse an extensive bibliography on the Brief Therapy Practice website at www.brieftherapy.org.uk which gives a link to the Brief Therapy Press at www.btpress.co.uk

You could start with an easy read and a broad-based introduction *Problem to Solution - Brief Therapy with Individuals and Families* by Evan George, Chris Iveson and Harvey Ratner. There are case studies showing the effectiveness of a solution focus with children, families and individuals and a chapter describing SFBT in a London comprehensive school.

Education-focused applications are described in *Solutions in Schools: Creative Applications of Solution Focused Brief Thinking with Young People and Adults* edited by Yasmin Ajmal and Ioan Rees. They offer a collection of presentations on, for example, stuck cases, anti-bullying, working with the secondary school system, counselling, the home–school interface, making the best use of time and students as a resource.

Berni Stringer and Madan Mall's manual *A Solution Focused Approach to Anger Management with Children* (Questions Publishing Company) gives practical guidance on setting up and running groups to support pupils with managing anger. Berni and Madan are experienced social workers who have worked extensively with children with disruptive and difficult behaviour. Their book presents a range of tried and tested exercises, which can be photocopied for use with groups or individuals. Helpfully, the manual is designed to be used by those with no prior knowledge of solution focused work! An online catalogue is at www.questionsonline catalogue.co.uk.

Another book giving a number of ready-planned sessions for use in school is *Confidence, Assertiveness and Self Esteem: For Secondary Pupils* written by Tina Rae and published by Lucky Duck. This 12-session course for secondary pupils teaches skills and strategies for more effective relationships and interactions at home and in school. It comes with a CD for easy production of appropriate materials. Here is the link to the Lucky Duck webpage again, www.luckyduck. co.uk.

Sometimes by yourself you just can't seem to get anywhere with a difficult youngster. *Circles of Adults* is a brilliant book describing 'a team approach to problem solving around challenging behaviour and emotional needs'. Derek Wilson and Colin Newton give clear instructions to guide you through a 10-step process targeted at changing thoughts and feelings around a particular young person or difficult issue. The book is one of many resources published by Inclusive Solutions, the Nottingham-based group of educational psychologists. A full catalogue can be seen at www.inclusive-solutions.com.

Session record sheet

Pupil .... Date of session ....

☐ Not You Again!

☐ What Else Can I Do With You?   Worksheet number

☐ Just Stop ... and Think!

Worksheet title....................................Staff initials..

Key points from this session

Actions for staff (What? Who? When?)

Issues for exploration at a future session

Review of progress made in this area   Date ....

Helping youngsters to understand their own behaviour

'The more you tramp on a cow pat the bigger it gets!'

In other words ... don't make your problems worse than they already are.

What do you do that makes your problems worse? Perhaps you answer back or sigh loudly or use a sarcastic tone of voice.

If you stopped doing these things how do you think your teacher would feel?

How would you feel?

What would your friends think?

Your name _____   Helper's name _____

Wheel of life

This chart will help you focus on 6 areas: perhaps 6 different lessons, 6 times of the day, 6 situations. Write the heading for each area in the shaded sections.

Now starting in the centre shade the bands according to how comfortable you feel with each area. More shaded bands = more comfortable.

In the sections outside the bands write what you will be doing differently when you feel you can shade the next band.

Think about how things will be when you can shade all the bands.

Your name _____

Helper's name _____

Person spec.

When jobs are advertised a person specification is written to make it clear what kind of person is needed.
What kind of person do you need to be to fill the job of 'successful pupil' at school?

Job title: **Successful pupil at school**   full / ~~part~~-time
~~temporary~~ / permanent

Essential characteristics, skills and knowledge.

Desirable characteristics, skills and knowledge

I will

Try to .... (Target)

Keep trying for .... (Time scale)

Keep this chart to show how well I am doing

Date	Oh dear! 😦	Nearly 😐	Hurrah! 😊	Comments

Your name _____   Helper's name _____

Are you in a fog?

On a sunny day we can see clearly all round us. If it is misty we might need to look more carefully but if it is foggy it can be almost impossible to see where you are going. It can be a bit scary too.

How are things for you?

Watch it

I am going to find out what I do that is causing a problem.

I am going to circle the next number each time I ....
....
....

This is when I will start .... and finish ....

I guess I will circle up to about number ....

1	2	3	4	5	6	7	8	9	10
11	12	13	14	15	16	17	18	19	20
21	22	23	24	25	26	27	28	29	30
31	32	33	34	35	36	37	38	39	40
41	42	43	44	45	46	47	48	49	50

Now I know what I am doing, I am going to change by

Your name _____   Helper's name _____

A ... B ... C ...

Over the next few days look carefully at what happens around the times you get into trouble. Fill in this chart to help you focus on how to make some changes for the better.

When did it happen? Date/lesson/ time?	A What was happening **Around** you at the time?	B What was your **Behaviour** and what did you do?	C What were the **Consequences**? What happened next?

Your name _____   Helper's name _____

Time line

- How did you get here?
- What are the milestones along the way?
- Are there any places where you feel you might have taken a wrong turn?

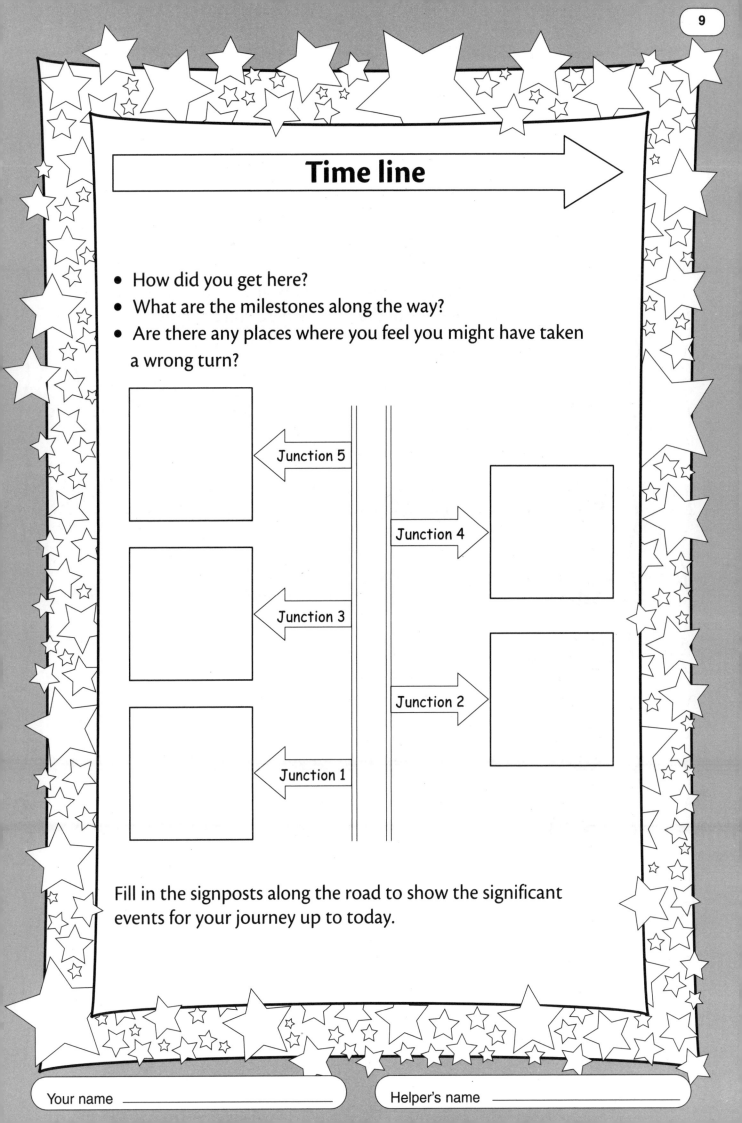

Junction 5

Junction 4

Junction 3

Junction 2

Junction 1

Fill in the signposts along the road to show the significant events for your journey up to today.

Your name _____

Helper's name _____

How low can you go?

Think about a time when things were worse than now, when things were as bad as they could be … the pits.

Now, before you get too depressed, think about what you have done to get yourself out of the pit to where you are now.

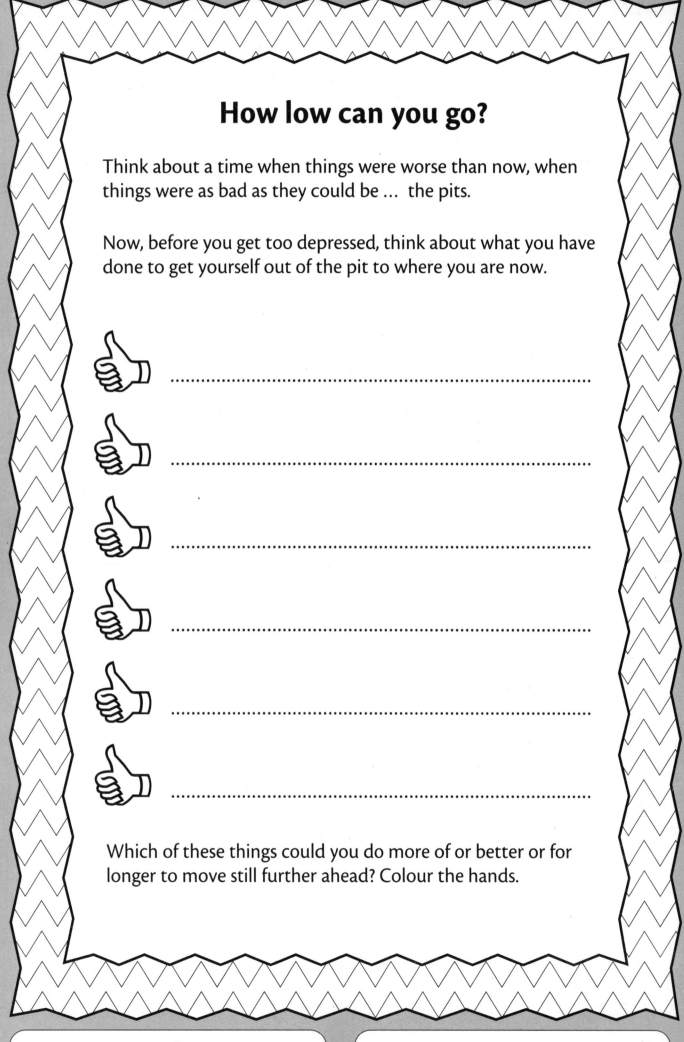

Which of these things could you do more of or better or for longer to move still further ahead? Colour the hands.

Your name _____

Helper's name _____

CV

Short for Curriculum Vitae which is Latin and means something like 'the plan of my life'.

When people apply for new jobs they send a CV to describe themselves. They write what they have done and what they are good at. Sometimes they give reasons why they should have the job. They give the name of someone who will recommend them for the job. This is called a reference.

Write a CV for the job of pupil in your school.

Name   DoB

My education so far:

Skills I have for the job:

Hobbies and interests:

My targets for the future in this job:

A reference can be obtained from:

Your name _____   Helper's name _____

Time out?

How much time do you spend on these things each day? You might need to add some more to the list. Colour more boxes for the things that take up more of your time.

Working

In good lessons

Messing about

With friends

Where should you make changes?
What will you do?

Archaeological dig

Archaeologists dig back through time to find out what life was like thousands of years ago. Can you think back just a short while to a time when things were better for you? What can you learn from that time that will help you get on better now?

Things were better when ...

At that time I did more of these things ...

And I did less of these things ...

It would help me now if I did more ...

And did less ...

Your name _____

Helper's name _____

Reflections

Describe the character of the person you see when you look in a mirror. Reflect on the good points, on the areas where this person needs to make some changes and what they have done to make a start on those changes.

Your name _____   Helper's name _____

MOT

Once cars are 3 years old they have to have an MOT – a test to see if they are OK to be on the road. Give your behaviour an MOT to see if you are OK to be in lessons.

	Passed	Needs servicing	Failed MOT	Areas for attention
English				
Maths				
Science				
Technology				
History/ geography				
Languages				
PE / sport				
Art / drama				

Mechanic's comments

Signed   Date of MOT

Your name _____   Helper's name _____

You're a star

Everyone has lots of good points. What have you done well recently to try to improve your behaviour? Write these things on the star.

What do you need to do make your star shine even more brightly?

Your name _____   Helper's name _____

If the cap fits ...

What do others say about you?	What would you prefer them to say?

Are there any statements on the left that you feel pleased about?

Which of the statements on the right is the one you most want to come true?

Your name _____

Helper's name _____

Helping youngsters to see others' point of view

No smoke without fire!

Have you heard this saying? It means that others see the smoke the problem is creating and even if they can't see the fire, the cause of the problem, they know it must be there.

What do others see of your difficulties? Make notes in the smoke.

Have a think about what is keeping the fire going. How could it be put out?

Your name _____   Helper's name _____

Fly on the wall

Imagine you are a fly on the wall at school watching what goes on.

- What do different people think of your behaviour?
- What do they think you could do to improve?
- Why do they think you get into trouble?

Use the chart below to record what other people might think as they buzz round school watching you. You might imagine the flies to be some of these:

| Friends | Girls | Teachers | Boys |
| Other adults in school | Younger pupils | Family | Older pupils |

Put somone's name and what they think by each of these 3 flies.

Your name _____   Helper's name _____

Opposites

Think of some words that describe your behaviour and note them down in the boxes on the left hand end of each line.

Now put the opposite of each word in the box at the right hand end of each line.

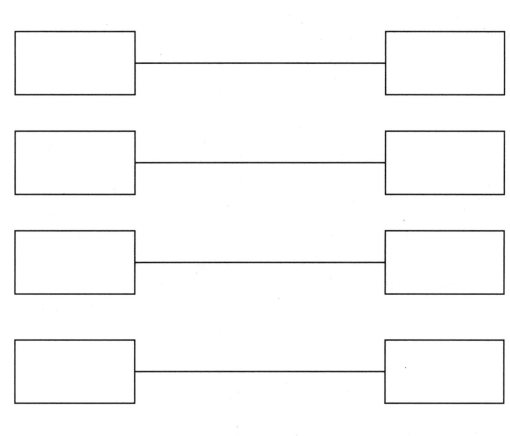

Put a mark on each line to show how near either end you feel you are. Where do teachers, friends and family see you? Choose different colours to show where they would put you on the line.

Can you put a star on each line to show where you would like to be?

Your name _____   Helper's name _____

10 things . . .

I'm good at

-
-
-
-
-
-
-
-
-
-

Adults say about me

-
-
-
-
-
-
-
-
-
-

Friends say about me

-
-
-
-
-
-
-
-
-
-

To change

-
-
-
-
-
-
-
-
-
-

Your name _____

Helper's name _____

Reputations

A reputation is often the first thing people hear about you. This seems to be particularly the case if you have often been in trouble ... people hear all the bad things about you before they even meet you. This changes the way they see you and what they think about you.

What sort of reputation do you have at school?

What would you like it to be?

What can you start to do today to give yourself a good reputation?

Who needs to notice the improvements you have made in your behaviour for your reputation to begin to change?

  Friends   Head teacher

☆ Other pupils   ☆ Deputy head

  Teachers   ☆ Family

Your name _____   Helper's name _____

Helping youngsters to
think about how the future might look

This Is Your Life!

If you were writing the chapter titles for a book about your life so far, what would they be? Thinking about significant events, turning points, failures or achievements may help you.

1.

2.

3.

4.

5.

What would you like the chapters to be called for your future? Think about changes you plan to make, where you see yourself in a year's time, what you would like to do when you leave this school.

6.

7.

8.

9.

10.

Can you think of a good title for your book?

Your name _____

Helper's name _____

Look to the future

A successful future may seem a long way off but it is there! If you could look through a telescope to make the future clearer what would you see yourself doing? Write or draw your ideas.

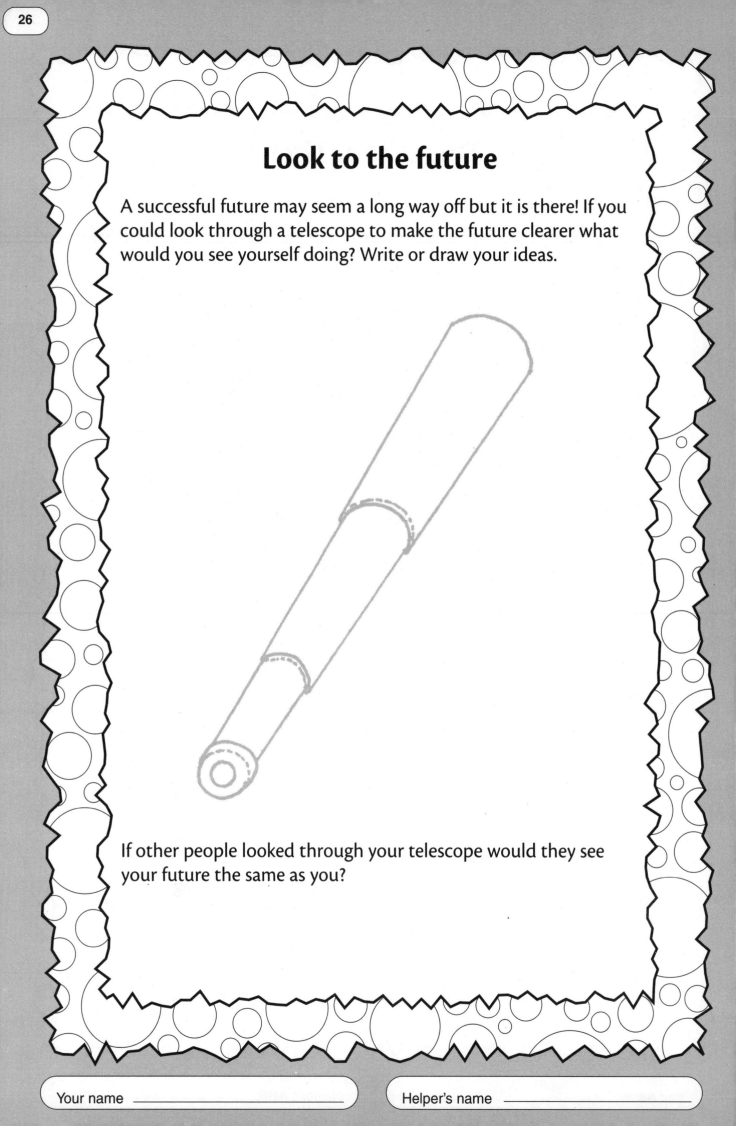

If other people looked through your telescope would they see your future the same as you?

Your name _____   Helper's name _____

Dream on

If my dreams came true …

Teachers would …	but would not …
My friends would …	but would not …
I would …	but would not …
My family would …	but would not …

What is the first thing you could do to start making your dreams come true?

Who would be the first to notice that things were changing for you?

Rose-tinted spectacles

Do you know what it means to see life through rose-tinted spectacles?

What would your life be like through rose-tinted spectacles?

What could you do to begin to make a difference?

Your name _____

Helper's name _____

The icing on the cake

What will be really, really good about when things are better?
Write these things in the jam and icing.

To make a good cake you need more than just jam and icing.
Make notes on the sponge cake of all the things that will be
different for you in the future.

What is the first ingredient for your cake?

Your name _____

Helper's name _____

Magic wand

If you could wave a magic wand over the situation in school what would happen?

These things would STOP happening

☆

☆

☆

These things would START happening

☆

☆

☆

These things would happen MORE

☆

☆

☆

Your name _____

Helper's name _____

Where next?

Where do you want to go after today?
How might you keep on the right road in future?
What will be the signposts to show that you are still on the
right road? Fill in the map.

Your name _____

Helper's name _____

Deal yourself a winning hand

In most card games there is some luck, but there is also skill.
If you had all four aces that would be as good a hand as you could usually get. Write what needs to happen for you to get four aces?

If you had a fifth ace up your sleeve, showing something you could do to make things almost perfect, what would it be?

Helping youngsters to consider the range of choices for action

Which way now?

You can make choices about your behaviour and where it will lead you. Think about some of the choices you could make now and put your 4 favourites round this chart.

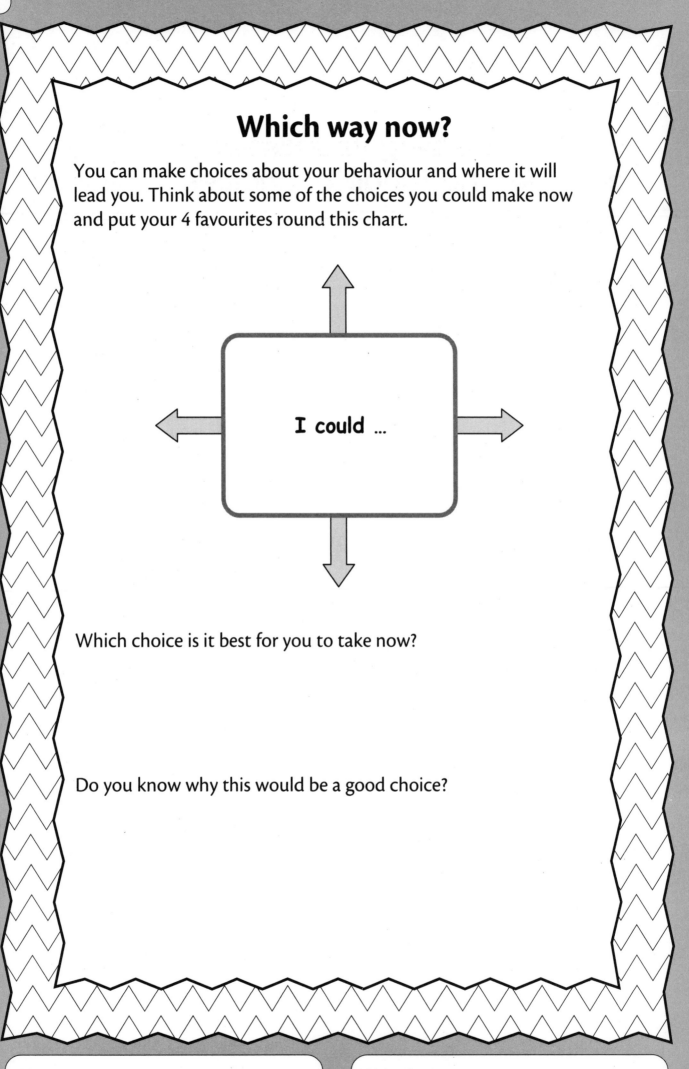

I could ...

Which choice is it best for you to take now?

Do you know why this would be a good choice?

Your name _____

Helper's name _____

Take the bull by the horns

What stops you making the changes you want?	How will you remove the barriers and make a start?

Your name _____

Helper's name _____

Stuck???

If you are really stuck for a first step to take to make things better think creatively.

Think about what these famous people do and what they are like. What would they suggest for your first step?

The Prime Minister and the Queen

☆ _____

☆ _____

Superman and Bart Simpson

☆ _____

☆ _____

Choose your own two famous characters or real people to help and note down the ideas they might give you.

☆ _____

☆ _____

Give all the new ideas a score out of ten for how much they might help you and write it in the star.

Your name _____   Helper's name _____

Still stuck?!

If you are still stuck for a way forward, or feel you would like some more ideas before you make a final decision about what you are going to do, think about how the following objects could give you a new idea. This is called *lateral thinking.* You may have to really rack your brains to come up with something different to try.

A bat

An egg

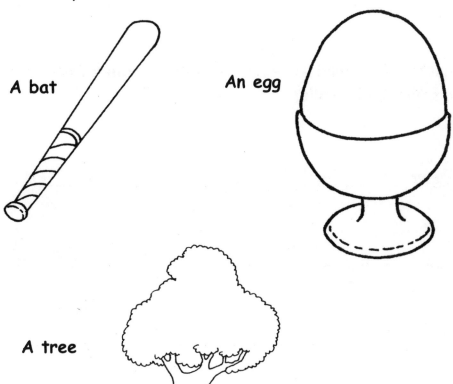

A tree

Have you got an idea to work on now? Make some notes so you don't forget.

Your name _____

Helper's name _____

Pack up your troubles

*'Pack up your troubles in your old kit bag
And smile, smile, smile.'*

This is a line from a song many older people will know.

What troubles need to be packed away in your kit bag to make you smile, smile, smile?

_____

_____

_____

_____

_____

Which will you work on first?

Your name _____   Helper's name _____

Mosaic

Tiny pieces of coloured stone or tile were put together by the Romans to make beautiful, intricately patterned floors.

Small pieces of behaviour can also be put together to make a picture of your behaviour.

What tiny changes will you make to design a better picture of yourself? Write them in the segments of the mosaic figure.

Your name _____

Helper's name _____

Juggling

It is hard to keep lots of juggling balls in the air at once and stop them falling all round you. What are all the things you need to do to stop things falling all round you?

Write some of them in the juggling balls.

Are you sitting comfortably?

Everyone is comfortable with some of the things they do – they are inside your comfort zone. To develop new skills or try new behaviours you have to step outside your comfort zone. This will be challenging and you might need practice and support to do these things. Think of one area you would like to change and write your thoughts in the outside zone.

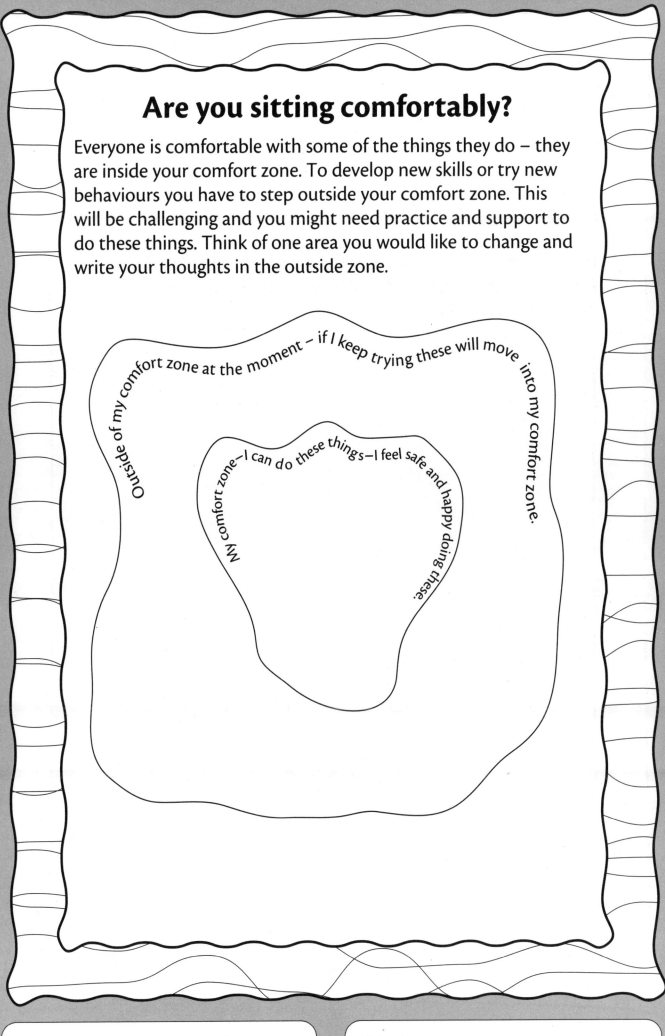

Outside of my comfort zone at the moment – if I keep trying these will move into my comfort zone.

My comfort zone – I can do these things – I feel safe and happy doing these.

Your name _____

Helper's name _____

Plaits

Problems are never simple. There are often a number of different strands to them that get knotted together and are difficult to unravel. If you can separate the parts it's often easier to sort them one by one.

Have a think about the situation you are in. What are the different parts that need dealing with? Write them on the strands of this plait.

Up the creek!

Are you up a creek … without a paddle? If so you may feel well and truly stuck. If you were in a real canoe you would have to think really hard about how to help yourself even if you could still see the paddle floating just out of reach.

What could you do if you were stuck in a real canoe deep in the Amazon jungle? There might be piranhas in the water so watch out!

What can you do to get paddling along smoothly again at school?

Watch out for the piranha-type problems! What might they be?

Your name _____   Helper's name _____

Diamond nine

Talk with someone about what is really important to you
or what you need to change
or things to help you
or things you are going to do.

Arrange nine of your ideas in a diamond shape. Put the most important, the vital, the essential thing in the top space. The bottom space is for the idea you are prepared to give up if you really must.

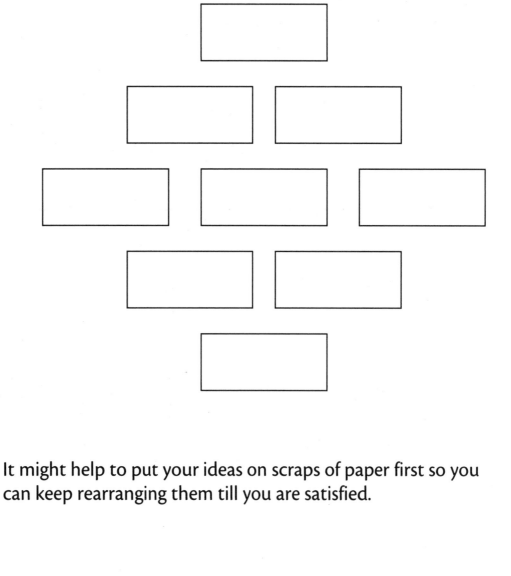

It might help to put your ideas on scraps of paper first so you can keep rearranging them till you are satisfied.

Your name _____   Helper's name _____

Helping youngsters to be aware of potential help and pitfalls

Banana skins

What could you slip up on the way to your goal?
Put a possible problem on each segment of the banana skin.

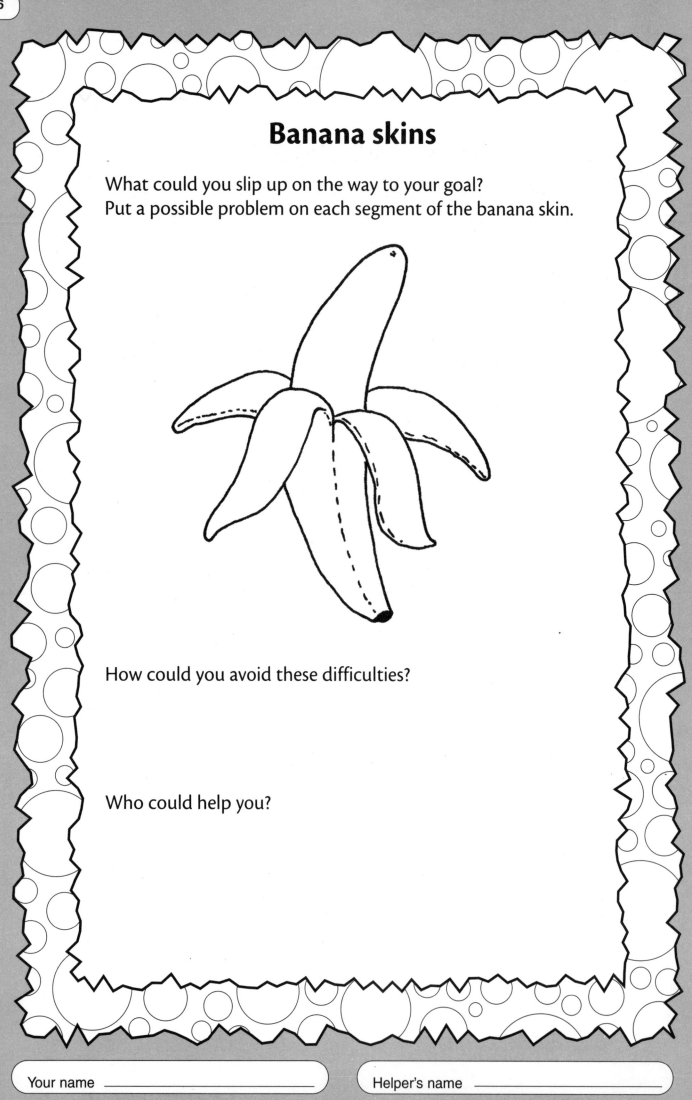

How could you avoid these difficulties?

Who could help you?

Your name _____   Helper's name _____

Peace summit

World leaders sometimes arrange a peace summit to try to sort out difficulties between countries. Who could help you begin to move forward and resolve your difficulties? Put their names round the globe.

Now set the agenda for the meeting. What 3 things should they help you with first?

1.

2.

3.

Your name _____   Helper's name _____

Every cloud
has a silver lining

Things may seem pretty bad at the moment but if you think hard there are bound to be some positive things that can take you forward.

- Perhaps someone is willing to help you sort things out
- Maybe you've now had a chance to talk through your difficulties
- Maybe you are a bit more determined to change now

Think really hard and talk to one of the staff to come up with some other positive and helpful things about the situation you are in. Make some notes here because it is these positive things that can be the first tiny steps to making things a lot better.

_____

_____

_____

_____

Your name _____   Helper's name _____

Half full or half empty?

It's good to try to look on the bright side, to be positive and to see the glass as half full. If you keep giving yourself positive messages things are likely to feel better.

Think now how you could put a positive spin on difficult situations you find yourself in.

I'm useless at maths.	I know more maths than I did last year.

Your name _____

Helper's name _____

Drain the swamps ... or trap the crocodiles?

Sometimes it's better to stop problems from even starting (that's the draining the swamp bit). Otherwise you have to sort the problem out once it has arisen (trap the crocodiles that live in the swamp you didn't drain!).

What could you do to drain the swamp?

-
-
-
-

What could you do to trap the problem once it has arisen?

-
-
-
-

Full speed ahead

Imagine the speed limit for making changes to your behaviour is 70 mph. So 70 mph is when you are trying the very, very best you can.

Put in the needle to show how fast you are making changes now.

What would help you get you going:

1 mph faster? ....

....

10 mph faster? ....

....

Up to the speed limit? ....

....

Your name _____   Helper's name _____

If at first you don't succeed try, try, try again.

Long, long ago a man called Robert the Bruce was hiding from his enemies. Whilst he was waiting for it to be safe to leave he watched a spider try over and over again to spin the first thread of a web. Eventually the spider was successful and spun a web. Robert the Bruce realised from this he should not give up too easily.

Now things are really hard for you what could you do to try, try, try again?

 _____

 _____

 _____

Who might be able to give you a helping hand, like the spider did for Robert the Bruce? What would you like them to do?

Your name _____   Helper's name _____

Shark attack

What is in the treasure chest that you really want to get? You can dive for sunken treasure but you must watch out for the sharks that want to stop you getting there.

On the treasure chest write your target. On the sharks write the problems you think you might face. Talk with someone about how you could swim round them.

Your name _____   Helper's name _____

Obstacle course

An obstacle course can be difficult but when you get to the end you can feel a great sense of achievement. Sorting things out at school will also be challenging but well worth doing.

Write what you would like to achieve by the finish line and label some of the obstacles you may face along the way.

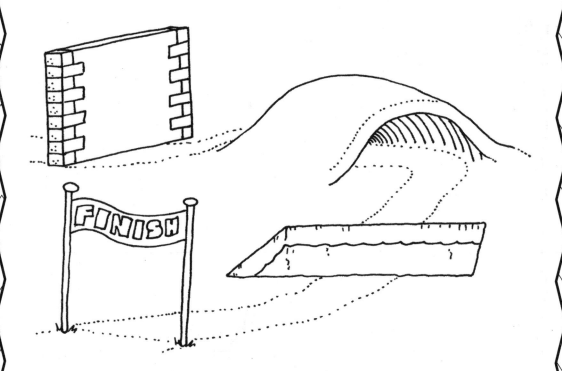

Is there a way to the finish line avoiding some of the obstacles?

Your name _____   Helper's name _____

Help!!

It's OK to ask for help. You wouldn't be working here now if people weren't willing to help you.

How could these people help you sort things out?

Family

Friends

Teachers

Tick one thing in each group that you are going to ask someone to do today to help you.

Your name _____

Helper's name _____

Radar

A radar is an early warning system. It helps air traffic controllers guide aeroplanes safely in to land. It would be useful to have a radar system round school to warn you of problems ahead, so you can avoid getting into trouble.

What are the potential trouble spots you need an early warning system for? Write them on the radar.

Here are some ideas to help if you get stuck:

- Times of the day
- Parts of the building you might be in
- People you may be with
- Different lessons
- How you feel at different times

Snakes and ladders

In the game of snakes and ladders the snakes drag you down and the ladders help you on up to the top. Can you fill in the snakes and ladders on this board with examples of the things that help you up and the things that might drag you down?

Remember you can be a winner.

Your name _____   Helper's name _____

Helping youngsters to plan a course of action

Traffic lights

Make some notes in each section.

STOP

Think about exactly what the problem is.

GET READY

What could you do to move forward?

GO

What are you going to do first?

Now go for it!

Your name _____   Helper's name _____

Sort it

It is often difficult to get started with something that is going to be hard to do. It can help to break the task up into smaller steps.

Note down what you are going to do to start helping yourself and when you will do it by.

I will...

    by.................................

I will...

    by.................................

I will...

    by.................................

What will be the first thing you will notice that will tell you that things are improving?

Your name _____ Helper's name _____

Another brick in the wall

You could look at this sheet in two ways. You might feel that you are trapped behind a brick wall and need to break out … Or you might feel that the situation you are in is falling apart and you need to build up a solid wall again.

Put an arrow between these walls to show which way you feel you need to move.

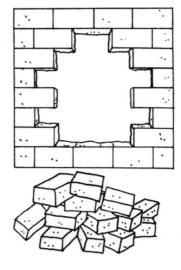

What are <u>you</u> going to do to get started? Write one action for each brick.

....

....

....

....

How will you know when the wall is as you would want it to be?

Your name _____   Helper's name _____

Countdown

Start preparing for take-off on your mission by making a ten-point plan. Remember that each line of the countdown should be an important part of your overall mission.

My mission is to . . .

10 _____

9 _____

8 _____

7 _____

6 _____

5 _____

4 _____

3 _____

2 _____

1 _____

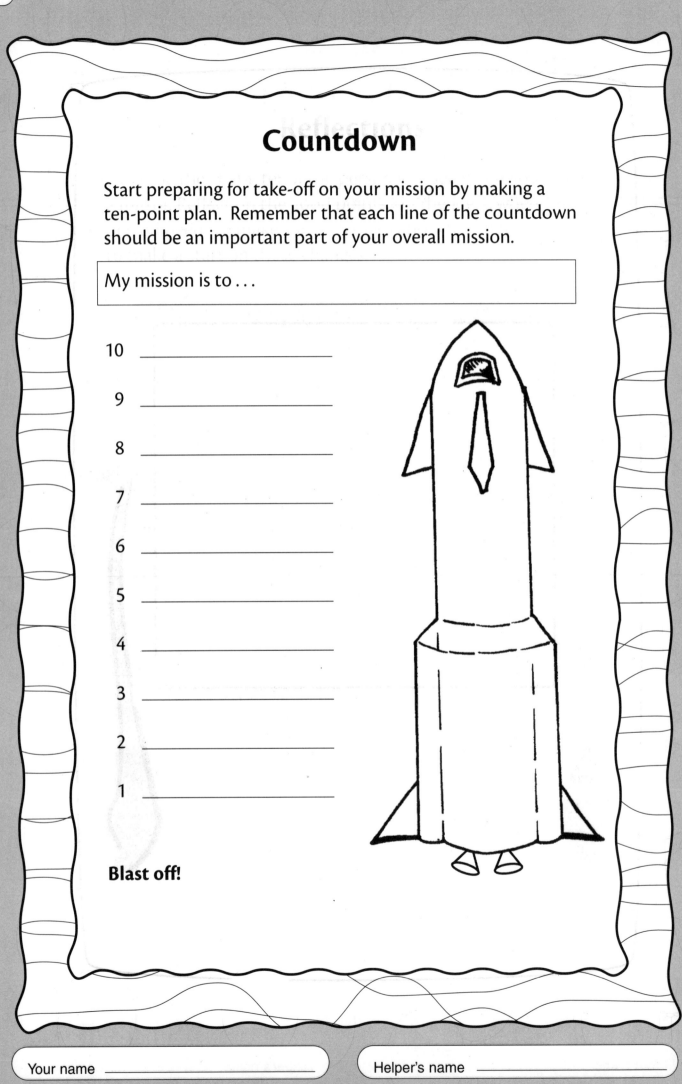

Blast off!

Raise the bar

Great athletes can jump over a bar set higher than 2 metres. That is certainly much too much of a challenge for nearly everyone else ... but you could set your own challenge and work toward it.

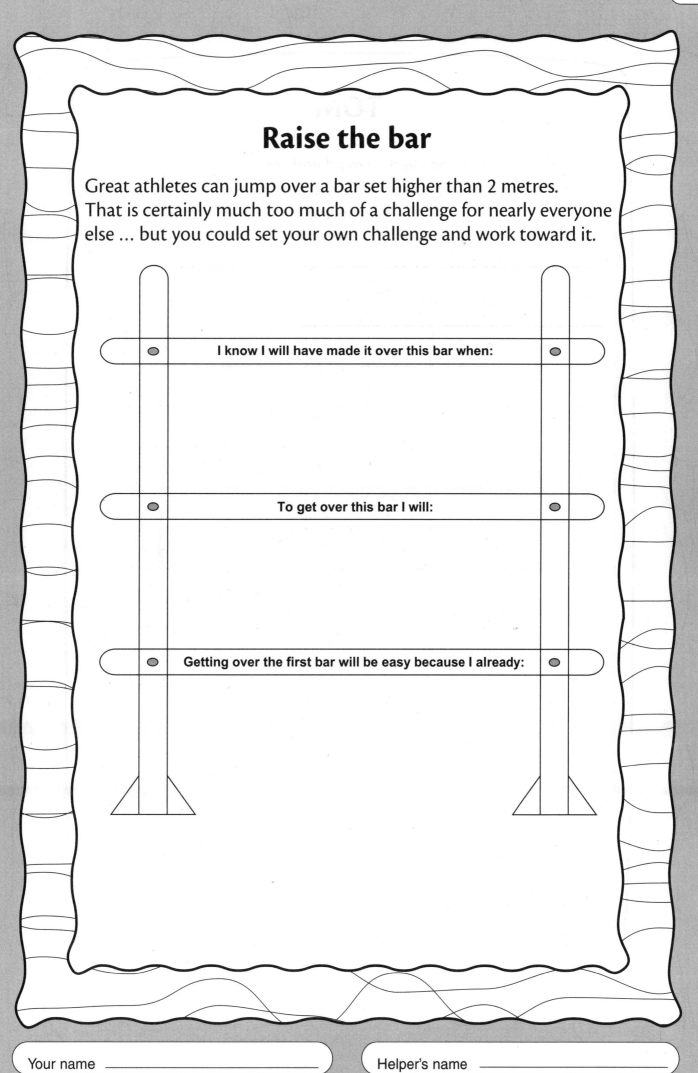

I know I will have made it over this bar when:

To get over this bar I will:

Getting over the first bar will be easy because I already:

Your name _____

Helper's name _____

Abracadabra

Make a magic spell to help you get rid of your difficulties.
Put all the things you need to do into the cauldron.

What would it be best to do first? Number the ingredients in
the order you plan to put them into action.

Your name _____   Helper's name _____

Go for gold

You may feel that you are able to go for gold straight away but it might not be easy. Give yourself some help by awarding yourself a bronze and a silver medal for achievements along the way.

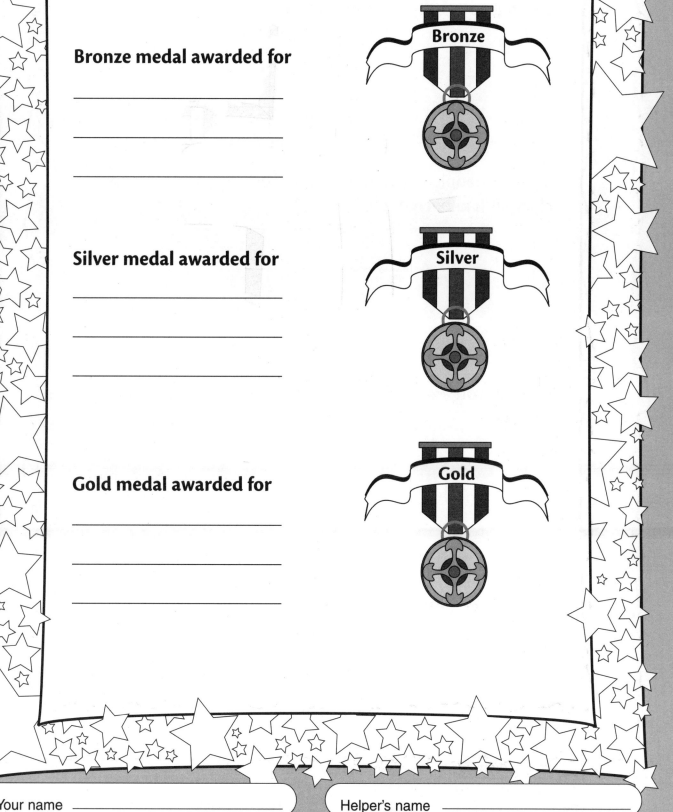

Bronze medal awarded for

_____

_____

_____

Silver medal awarded for

_____

_____

_____

Gold medal awarded for

_____

_____

_____

Your name _____

Helper's name _____

2 4 6 8
Who do we appreciate?!

To get people to 'appreciate' you more see if you can come up with:

2 things you really need to change.

4 things people would notice that were different once these changes had been made.

6 things you are going to do this week to begin to make things change.

8 days from now get back together with the person who is supporting you and review how things are progressing.

Your name _____   Helper's name _____

Cool it

What is the worst your behaviour has been?
How hot did it get?

Mark a red line on the thermometer to show this.

Put a blue line to show the calmest and coolest you have been.

What is the temperature now?

What needs to happen to reduce the temperature by

10°

20°

30° ... or back to the coolest it has been?

How will you know when things have cooled down
again to a more comfortable temperature?

Keep on up

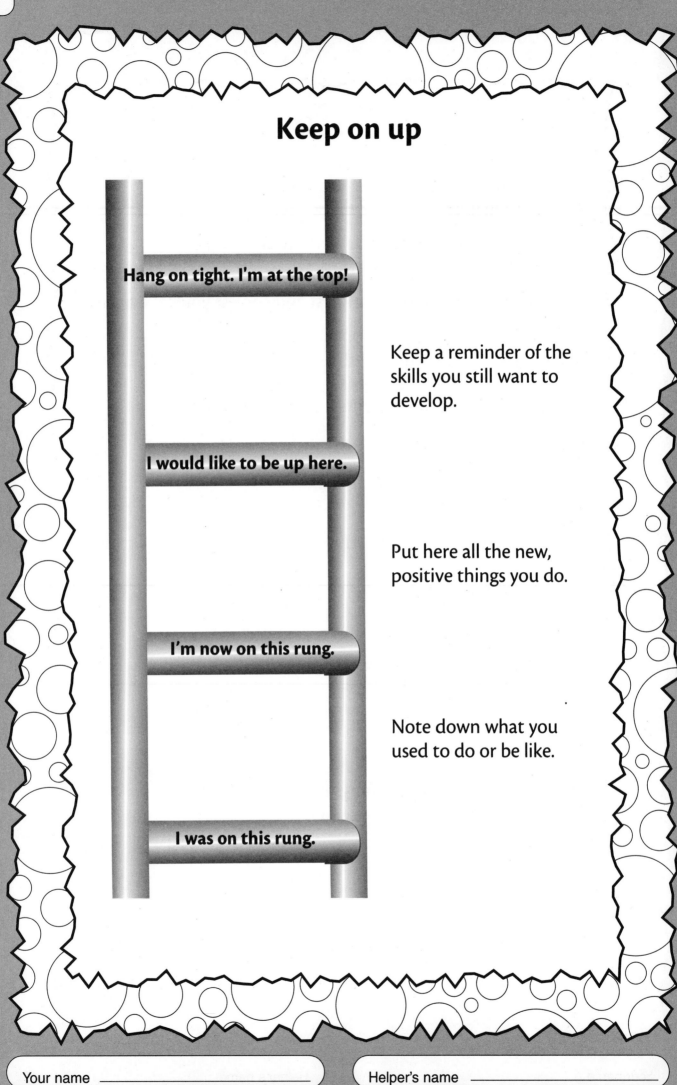

Keep a reminder of the skills you still want to develop.

Put here all the new, positive things you do.

Note down what you used to do or be like.

Your name _____

Helper's name _____

Plan – Do – Review

Your teachers will know all about the 'Plan – Do – Review' cycle. They will often use it to help them improve the way things are in school. You can use it too!

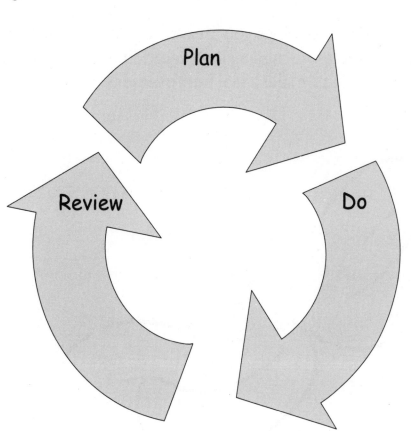

Fill in the **Plan** and **Do** arrows and remember to keep the sheet so that you can use it at the review meeting.

Review

How did you get on? What will you do differently? Will you need a new plan? Fill in the arrow.

Your name _____   Helper's name _____

The missing link

You will already be doing much to improve your behaviour but there are probably one or two things more you could still do. These may well be the vital missing links!

Write in some of the things you are already doing to help yourself. Complete the missing links by adding in two things you could begin to do to make a real improvement in how others see your behaviour.

To make sure the chain does not fall apart it needs to be soldered or welded together. What can you do to make sure your new links do not come apart?

Your name _____   Helper's name _____

On your bike

Can you remember how hard it was to learn to ride a bike? You will have been a bit wobbly at the start but after lots of practice you will have been able to ride along in a straight line. After even more practice you will have been able to ride round things that got in your way. To learn each new skill you need to be pretty good at the one before.

Improving your behaviour is a bit like learning to ride a bike. If you keep trying you get better and better. Once you have mastered one step you can move onto the next. Fill in the chart to show the things you need to do to improve your behaviour.

Riding a bike	Improving behaviour
learn to balance	
learn to use brakes	
ride in a wobbly line	
ride in a straight line	
ride round obstacles	

Your name _____

Helper's name _____

Don't run before you can walk

You will not be able to remember learning to walk. It is something that will have taken lots of practice and you will have had lots of help from your family and from things like furniture to hold onto. Each part of the sequence has to be learned before you can do the next. For example, you can't walk till you can stand and you can't run until you can walk.

Fill in the steps to make you successful in school.

Learning to walk	Being successful in school
Sit up	
Crawl	
Move round holding on	
Walk holding hands	
Walk alone	
Run, jump, climb	
A successful mover	Successful in school

Your name _____

Helper's name _____

The acid test

Scientists dip litmus paper in a liquid to see how acid or alkaline it is. The paper changes colour and is compared against a chart to show what sort of liquid has been tested.

Make a colour chart for behaviour.

Now test your behaviour. Do it carefully, with thought and discussion. Colour your results on this test strip.

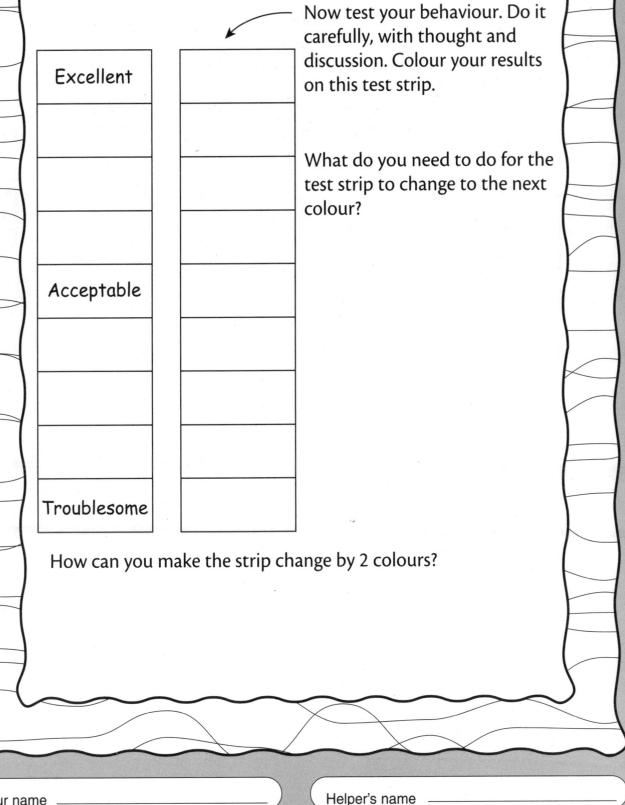

Excellent

Acceptable

Troublesome

What do you need to do for the test strip to change to the next colour?

How can you make the strip change by 2 colours?

Tomorrow is the first day of the rest of your life

Think about the title of this sheet. What do you really want to do with your life? <u>Now</u> is the time to start making those things happen.

A time when many people think about their future is on New Year's Eve. Resolutions are made for better behaviour in the next year. It isn't New Years Eve today but you could still make some 'New You' resolutions. What would they be?

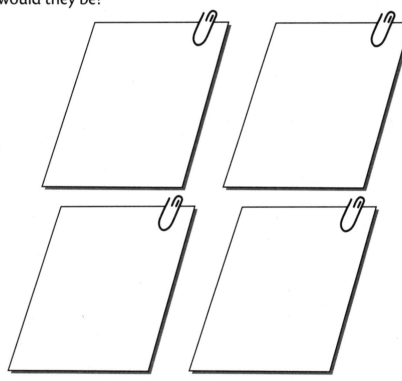

What will you do first to start making each of the changes?

● -   ● -

● -   ● -

Your name _____   Helper's name _____

Look before you leap

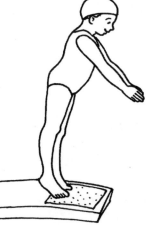

Take a careful look at where you plan to go before you dive in. Make sure you know about the hidden difficulties and have a way to deal with them before you encounter them.

This is where I want to go with my behaviour.

These are the difficulties I might come across.

These are ways I could avoid the problems happening at all.

These are the ways I could deal with the problems that do arise.

Your name _____   Helper's name _____

Experiment

When you write about a scientific experiment you put information under these headings

1. **Hypothesis** what you think might happen as a result of your experiment.

2. **Method** this describes exactly what you did.

3. **Results** this section describes what happened.

4. **Conclusion** here you say what you have learned from your experiment.

Try this as a way of experimenting with your behaviour to see what happens if you change some of the things you do.

Hypothesis

Method

Results

Conclusion

Your name _____

Helper's name _____

Marathon run

Running 26 miles takes a lot of preparation and determination. If you trained for a marathon you would run nearly every day, exercise all your muscles, eat a healthy diet and get lots of rest too. You would set yourself targets and build up to them. Improving your behaviour will also take preparation and determination. Decide on the milestones along your marathon route to your chosen finish line.

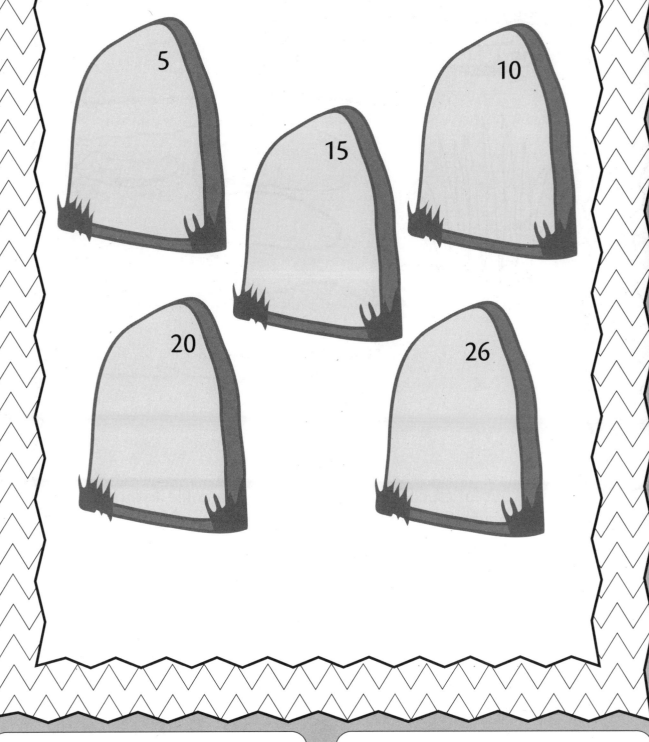

Stepping-stones

What will be your stepping-stones to get to a better situation on the other side of the river?

Write on each one.

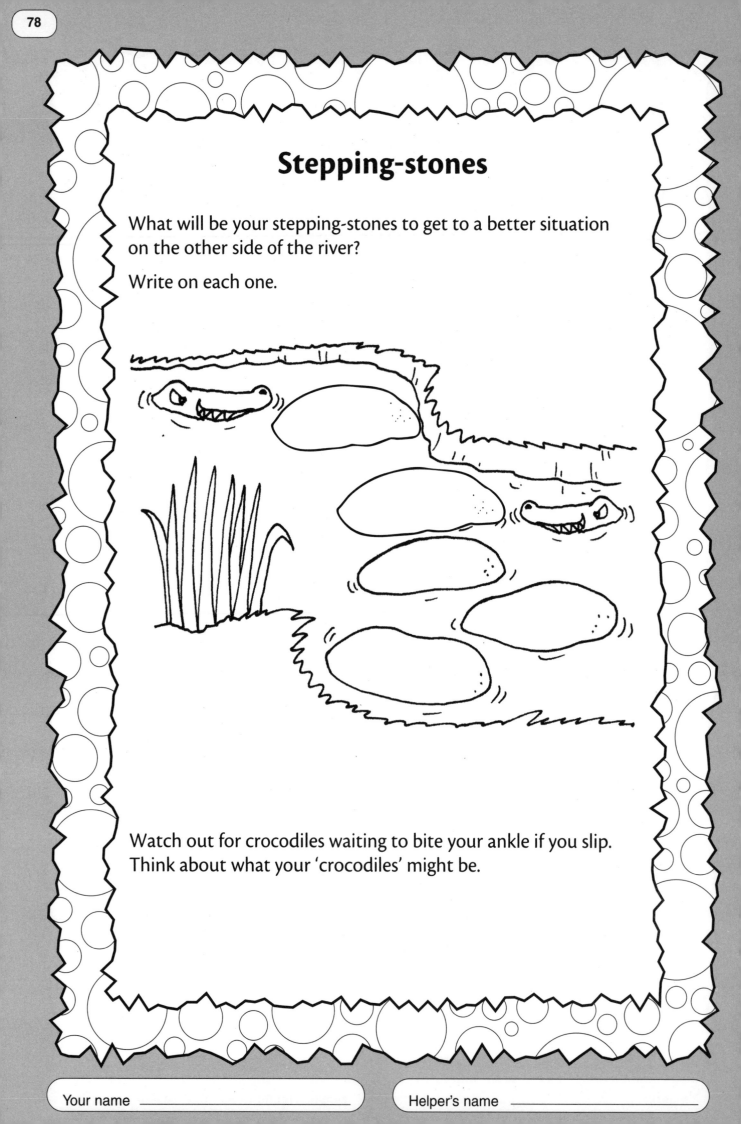

Watch out for crocodiles waiting to bite your ankle if you slip. Think about what your 'crocodiles' might be.

Your name _____   Helper's name _____

Helping youngsters to
check and review their progress

Pit stop

Grand Prix racing drivers get called into the pits part way through a race to check tyres and engines and fill up with fuel ready for the next laps.

While you work on your behaviour you will also need to make checks on how you are getting on. Use these questions to help you review your progress.

Have you stuck to your plan?

What has gone better or been easier than you expected?

Has there been anything that has been harder or has not gone so well?

What is still left to do to reach the chequered flag?

Your name _____

Helper's name _____

W W W

... not the World Wide Web, but

'What Went Well?'   and it would have been
even better if ...

What can you do about the 'even better ifs'?

-
-
-

Your name _____   Helper's name _____

On target

Bull's eye! These things went really well, better than I had expected.

On target. I'm pleased with each of these achievements.

Missed the target. I didn't quite make it in these areas and need a new plan for them.

Your name _____

Helper's name _____

Reports!

Write your own report of how you are getting on with improving your behaviour in lessons or around school. Give yourself a mark for effort and one for achievement. Write a comment saying what you need to do next.

Subject	Effort	Achievement	Comment

Overall good progress has been made especially in

More effort needs to be made with

Your name _____

Helper's name _____

How am I doing?

Choose the areas you are going to review. Write them in the boxes along the bottom. Fill in the bar chart to show how you are doing.

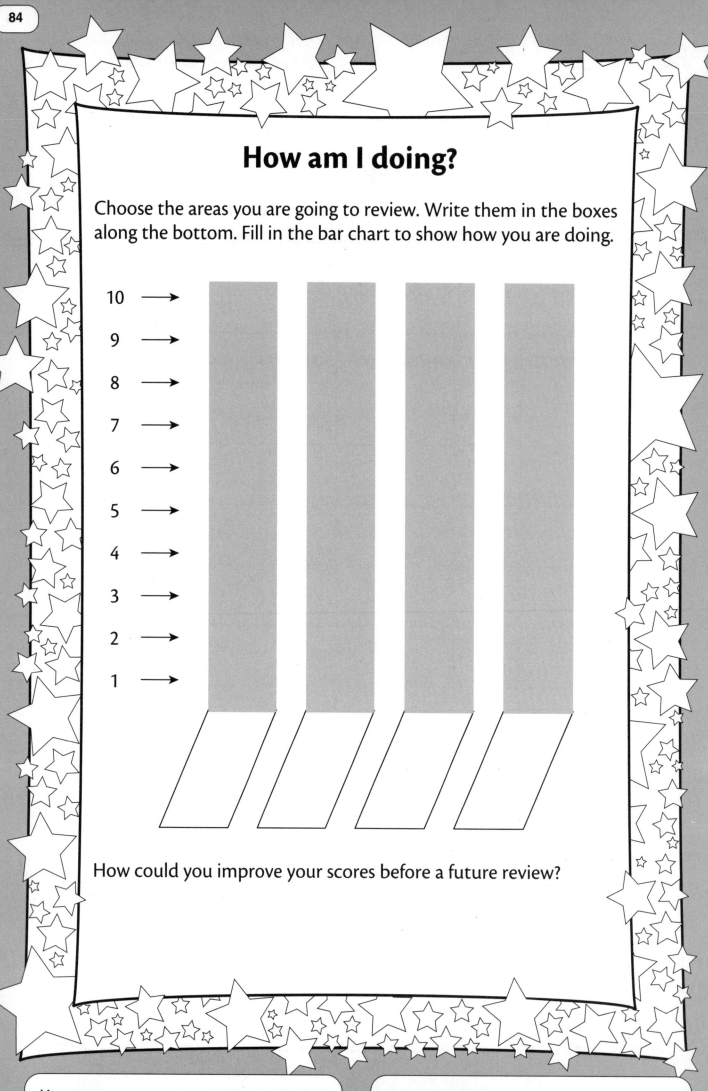

10 ⟶
9 ⟶
8 ⟶
7 ⟶
6 ⟶
5 ⟶
4 ⟶
3 ⟶
2 ⟶
1 ⟶

How could you improve your scores before a future review?

Your name _____

Helper's name _____

Market research

To get a full picture of how well you are doing you might need to ask other people. Finish writing this short questionnaire. Photocopy it and do your market research.

1. What changes do you see in me?

2. How hard do you think I have tried?

   not at all   not much   quite hard   really hard   the best you can

3.

4.

5.

Remember to thank the person for answering your questionnaire.
Put their name here..........................

Your name _____   Helper's name _____

Your name _____

Helper's name _____

Your name _____

Helper's name _____

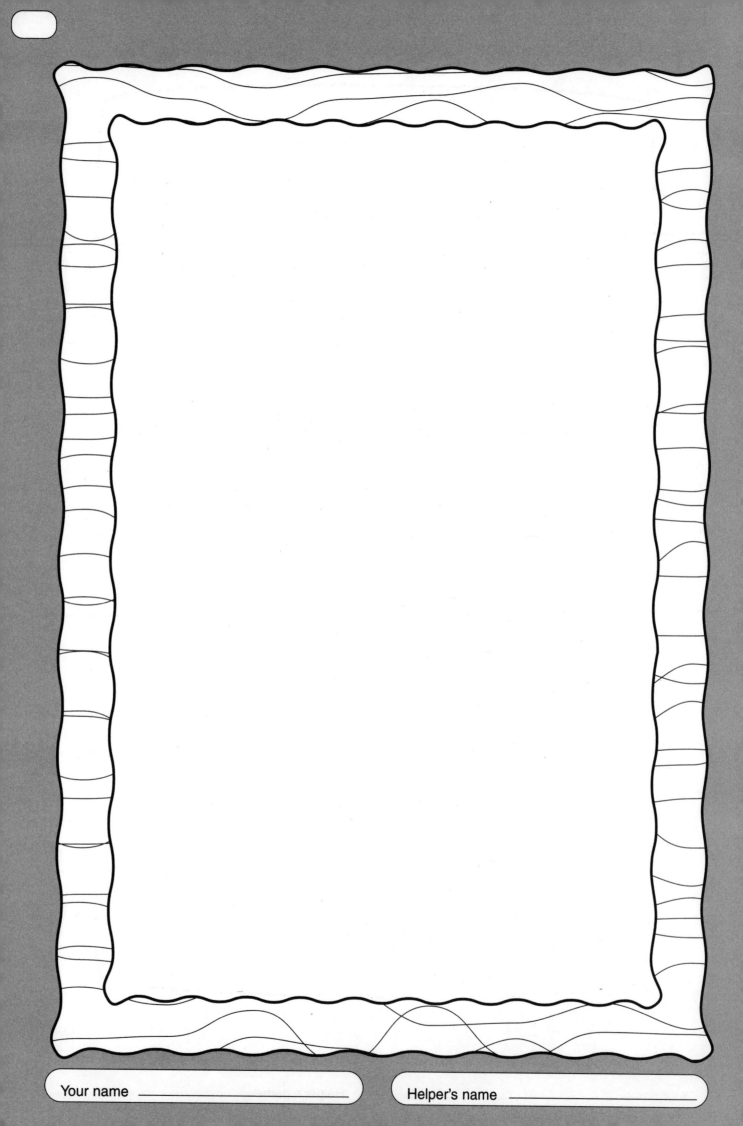

Your name _____

Helper's name _____

Your name _____

Helper's name _____

Your name _____

Helper's name _____